A guide and short history of
DEANS COURT

The oldest house in Wimborne, Dorset

Janet K L Seal

Best Wishes!

Janet K L Seal

Wimborne History Publications

ISBN 978-0-9954523-0-5

First published 2016
ISBN 978-0-9954523-0-5
© 2016 Janet K L Seal - All rights reserved

Acknowledgements

The historic portraits and paintings on pages 7, 10, 11, 17, 20, 21, 26 and 28
and the photographs on the cover and pages 4, 12, 15, 16, 25, 27, 29 and 31 were
supplied by Sir William Hanham, the photograph on page 13 supplied by
Bristol Museums and the remainder by the author Janet K L Seal.

Published by Wimborne History Publications

Printed in Great Britain by Booths Print, Penryn, Cornwall

Welcome to Deans Court

My family has lived at Deans Court for 470 years. During this time the house has undergone many changes and survived many periods of social, economic and religious upheaval. In common with many estates, the succession has not followed a direct path, but nonetheless 14 generations of Hanhams have loved and cared for this place. Since I succeeded my father in 2009, my wife Alison and I have launched various initiatives to help with the upkeep of the house, the garden and its buildings, in the hope that Deans Court remains as relevant and central to the community of Wimborne as it has for the last 1,300 years. I trust this guide will bring to life the many centuries of history that can be found at Deans Court.

Sir William Hanham, 13th Baronet

A visitor to Deans Court enters a building that reflects the past through many centuries. From Saxon times when it was part of a double monastery ruled by a royal abbess, to the latest improvements in 1868, history is hidden behind the elegant brick façade.

A high quality stone building stood on this site from 705AD. The nunnery housed both monks and nuns surrounded by 'high and stout' walls, their land including all the eastern part of Wimborne, the southern slopes of Colehill and the town mill on the River Wym, now the Allen. They sent missionaries to the continent and stories of the female pope coming from Wimborne, and the kidnapping of a nun in Saxon times, have some basis in fact.

Generations of Cerdician Saxon kings supported the religious house which was so close to their own palace at Pamphill, North West of Wimborne.

1. Deans Court House. 2. The Leaze. 3. The Minster. 4. Colehill, on rising ground.
5. The two streams of the River Allen.

The town was razed to the ground in 1015AD by raiding Danes, the nuns taken for high value virgin slaves and many of the monks killed. The jewels in the covers of the beautiful handwritten gospels produced by the nuns were probably picked out with daggers, the books discarded. For thirty years the buildings stood deserted, roofless and desolate, populated only by the ghosts of their former residents.

It was not until 1043AD that King Edward 'the Confessor' re-named the church St Cuthburga's and transformed the nunnery lands into a Deanery, appointing a personal friend to this position, that the walls were used once again.

Each king in turn appointed the Dean of Wimborne. They often had several positions of importance. In 1200 the Dean appointed by King John was Amaury de Harcourt. Finding that his own profitable market would be in competition with that of the lord of Kingston, a new village of thirty to forty properties was built on the Leaze, Deanery land, and occupied by well-to-do artisans. The depressions and platforms left behind can still be seen today.

One Dean, appointed on 12th April 1265 was John de Kirkby, head of King Henry III's tax collecting department. Needless to say, he was not popular!

When plague came to England in 1347 over half the population died and were buried in a nearby churchyard, now the Square. Wimborne was almost deserted and many houses were now empty. Those who survived moved closer to the church leaving the houses and cottages on the Leaze to decay.

Dean Gilbert Kymer in 1426 was actually the king's doctor, another was a judge at the assize courts. The Church or Consistory court had the power to chastise people who refused to attend church or behaved badly. It was held in the North east part of the Minster.

Dean William Smith (1485-92) a royal official, was closely associated with both Margaret Beaufort and King Henry VII. The former was the daughter of John Beaufort, owner of Kingston Hall (now Kingston Lacy) once a royal palace, where he committed suicide. A later Dean, Hugh Oldham, became her personal chaplain and was instrumental in founding the grammar school.

In 1518 Reginald Pole was appointed Dean of Wimborne by King Henry VIII even though he was not a priest and was still in his teens! Queen Mary appointed him Archbishop of Canterbury.

Leland's visit to Wimborne in the mid 1530s notes that there was a Dean, 4 prebendaries, 3 vicars, 4 deacons and 5 singing men. The vicars are thought to have had houses in the town but that still leaves fourteen people to be accommodated in the Deanery.

When King Henry VIII died he left a young boy, an ardent Protestant, as the next ruler. King Edward VI had the Deanery and College of Canons closed down. A group of Commissioners including John Hannam, then MP for Poole, was sent to Wimborne in 1548 to confiscate the Minster lands. The Chantries were dissolved and since that of Lady Margaret Beaufort paid for a school master to teach grammar, the school too, was forced to close.

The Hanham Family History

John Hannam, married Alice 'de Orange' in 1548, a wealthy Wimborne lady. He now had the opportunity to buy the Deanery lands and other properties belonging to Wimborne Minster and the Dean, which of course included the Dean's House or court.

John Hannam 1548

Set back from East Street almost due south of the Minster, the Dean's house had a large hall, a solar or upstairs room for his own use and lodging for the canons, priests and singing boys, as well as servants. As with many houses the kitchens were built separate from the main house for safety reasons.

The Dean would undoubtedly have owned several horses and sumpter ponies to carry his possessions so stabling, a feed room and basic accommodation for his groom and the stable boys might have been built into the eaves.

Abridged family tree of the Hanham family showing the descent from ancient times and the holders of the baronetcy.

William Hanam **=** Margaret dau of John Longe
of Horsington of Purse Caundle
d. 1505 *m. 1487, d. pre-1505*

Richard Hanam/ Hannam **=** Ricarda dau of John
40 or more January 1528/29 Triptrye of Somerset
when he inherited ⅓ share of *m.c. 1510*
Purse Caundle estate *d. 25 July 1549*

John Hannam of Deans Court **=** Alice dau of William Orange
Wimborne Minster of Wimborne Minster
MP for Poole 1547 *d. 1560*
d. 9 September 1559

Richard Hannam Thomas Hannam **=** Penelope dau of Sir
17 at 10 Oct 1559 Sgt at Law John Popham, Lord
m. pre November 1565 9 May 1589 Chief Justice. *d.1621*
d. November 1572. *d. 30 August 1593*
Heir d. aged 13

Sir John Hanham, Thomas Hanham **=** Elizabeth Broughton
Kt. High Sheriff of Dorset 1614 *b. 1576 d. 1652*

John Hanham **=** Frances dau of
Francis Dodington

Sir William Hanham **=** Elizabeth dau of
m. January 1665/6 George Cooper of
1st Baronet Clarendon Park, Wilts,
24 May 1667 niece of 1st Earl of
d. 20 May 1671 Shaftesbury
d. 1721/2

Sir John Hanham **=** Jane dau & heir of
2nd Baronet William Eyre of
bapt 21 July 1668 Neston Park, Wilts
bur 24 September 1709 *bur 19 August 1707*

Sir William Hanham **=** Mary dau of
3rd Baronet William Norris
b.c. 1694 of Nonsuch, Wilts
d. 28 March 1762 *d. 24 December 1774*

8

Rev Sir James
6th Baronet
b. 1725/6
Rec W'bourne
Zelston
1754-1800.
d. 11 Mar 1806

= Jane niece &
sole heir of
Wm Phelips
of Corfe
Mullen
m. 6 Sept 1757
bur 7 August
1783

Anne (1) dau
of James
Jennings of
Shiplake,
Oxon
m. 1744/5
d.s.p. 22 Sept
1756

= Sir William
Hanham
4th Baronet
Lt Col Dorset
Militia DL
Dorset
d. 11 Feb 1776

= (2) Mary dau
of V. Rev
William
Lynch
m. 2 June 1762
bur 23 October
1764

Sir William Thomas Hanham
5th Baronet
b. June 1763.
bur 18 August 1791

Ann (1) dau of
Edward Pike RN
m. 16 April 1793
d. 15 July 1801

= Rev Sir James
7th Baronet
b. 10 Mar 1760
Rector W'bourne
Zelston 1800-49
d. 2 Apr 1849

= Eliza Dean (2) dau
of Lt. William
Patey RN
m. 14 Dec 1815
d. 5 June 1877

Harriet dau of
George Morgan
m. 6 November 1823
d. February 1838

= Sir William
Hanham
8th Baronet
b. 7 May 1798
dsp 27 March 1877

Capt. John
Hanham
b. 14 Jan 1823
d. 16 Sept 1861

= Amy Ursula dau
of Alexander
Copland of
Winkfield Pl.,
Berks
m. 11 Aug 1853
m. (2) 1872
Camille Caillard, JP
d. 14 Jan 1909

Cordelia Lopes
dau of 1st Baron
Ludlow of
Heywood
m. 18 July 1896

= Sir John Alexander
Hanham
9th Baronet
b. 5 July 1854
d. 21 Feb 1911

Phelips Brooke
Hanham
b. 27 March 1858
d. 20 Feb 1917

= Gertrude dau of Lt
Col Patrick Paget
m. 9 Sept 1884
d. 16 Sept 1922

Sir John Ludlow
Hanham
10th Baronet
b. 23 Jan 1898
d. unm. 30 Apr 1955

Maud
b. 19 May 1899
d. unm. 19 Feb 1974

Sir Henry Phelips
Hanham
11th Baronet
b. 6 Apr 1901
d. unm. 23 Nov 1973

Dulcie dau of
William Daffarn
m. 14 Dec 1921
d. 15 Mar 1979

= Patrick John
Hanham
b. 16 Oct 1893
d. 23 Feb 1965

Margaret Jane dau
of Harold Thomas
b. 5 Oct 1931
d. 30 Oct 2007

= Sir Michael William
Hanham, DFC
12th Baronet
b. 31 Oct 1922
d. 30 May 2009

Victoria Jane
b. 8 Mar 1955

Sir William John
Hanham
13th Baronet
b. 4 Sep 1957

= Alison dau of
John Birch
b. 4 Jun 1961

Portrait of Alice de Orange, wife of
John Hannam, in the dining room, Deans Court

In 1554 the house now belonged to John Hannam, the third owner of a property on this site, each one incorporating much of what had been there before. The monastery fish pond remained and although the orchard had probably suffered from the ravages of time and lack of care this too was no doubt restored.

Marriage was akin to a business arrangement for the benefit of two families. The young couple would have met but love was not essential. What lands or dowry the bride's father provided with his daughter was just as important as the rank of the bridegroom and his prospects.

They had two sons, Richard and Thomas. When John died in 1559 his will set out the names of trusted gentlemen who would look after his son's estate until he gained his majority in April 1564. Meanwhile Richard qualified as a lawyer. He was later one of the Governors of the Free Grammar school in Wimborne when it was re-instated in 1563 by Queen Elizabeth I.

When Richard died in 1572 he asked Sir James Dyer, William James, Thomas Newton and his brother, to oversee his young son John who was only six years old at the time.

Thomas Hannam – Sergeant-at-Law

John never grew to maturity. Even though there was a daughter, the succession dictated that the estate had to be passed to a male heir. Deans Court therefore in 1579, was owned by Richard's younger brother, Thomas, who had also followed a legal career.

Thomas Hannam married Penelope, daughter of Sir John Popham, Lord Chief Justice of England in 1591. The career of the young man benefited from his father-in-law, rising in the legal profession and entering politics. Thomas died in 1593 leaving several children of whom John, the eldest son was his heir.

South lawn showing the two imported trees, both higher than Deans Court

The manors would be supervised by the executors of his will until John, who was only nineteen at his father's death, came of age and he could inherit an estate of 4000 acres. The young man was immediately taken under the wing of Sir John Popham but travelled before entering Parliament in 1601. Perhaps he was at St Cuthburga's church in Wimborne on the Sunday morning the previous year when the spire collapsed. It was deemed nothing short of a miracle that no-one was killed.

Being present at the coronation of King James I of England, VI of Scotland on 25th July 1603, John was one of the men knighted the same day. From then on he spelled the surname Hanham. He served a term as Sheriff of Dorset, was no doubt involved in the governing body of both the Royal Peculiar, the Minster church and the Queen Elizabeth free Grammar school in Wimborne which his father had built. An armorial window at Deans Court celebrates his work. He would also have been part of the welcoming committee when the King visited the town and the nearby estates of Kingston Hall and Cranborne.

Panel from the 267 foot New World Tapestry (1980-2000, Bristol Museums), showing Wimborne Minster, Thomas Hanham writing his journal and Martin Pring taking a sextant reading - Bristol Culture/Bristol Museum, Galleries & Archives/Design: Tom Mor ▶

His younger brother Thomas meanwhile pursued a career at sea. At the instigation of Sir John Popham, King James issued a charter in 1606 allowing an exploratory voyage to Virginia. The first ship was captured by the Spanish failing to make its rendezvous with the second ship commanded by Captain Thomas Hanham. A year later George Popham, nephew of Sir John, captained another ship, the Mary & John, and founded a colony in New England. Thomas brought back saplings, one Tulip tree and one Swamp Cypress which he planted in the grounds of Deans Court.

He also recorded the journey, the strange animals and the discovery of silver in a detailed diary. Apparently some of the details were so graphic that the printer stopped the publication and the diaries have since been lost.

Thomas Hanham's voyage is recorded in the world's longest tapestry which was created to mark the 400th anniversary of the Jamestown settlement.

When his brother, Sir John Hanham, died on 28th August 1625 leaving only one daughter, Thomas inherited Deans Court, the duties of the Lord of the Manor and all the other responsibilities of a major landowner.

The recent Visitation of the shire of Dorset by the Heralds in 1623 had set out the family tree to that date and verified the family right to its coat of arms.

There is one big difference between this one and that shown previously - the left glove, the sign that the bearer is a baronet has not yet been awarded to the family.

Coat of arms shown in its simplest form.

Henry Hanham, Thomas's younger brother was one of the 'upright men of the parish' elected to serve on the Board of Governors of the Grammar School. As part of his duties he would have sat in the Consistory court whose main function was to prevent immoral behaviour in Wimborne, to punish scolds, sellers of underweight loaves or imperfect goods at the town market.

Deans Court taken from hand drawn map in 1613 - Dorset History Centre.

Every town had its own stocks, pillory and ducking stool for the punishment of offenders.

Thomas Hanham (senior) died in August 1652 aged 76 having already attended the funeral of his second son, Thomas, aged only 33 years old. Both were buried in Wimborne Minster. He had a monumental inscription on an altar tomb of grey marble but this is no longer there.

Thomas Hanham memorial in Wimborne Minster.

North front of Deans Court

The Thomas Hanham memorial with the colourful armorial shields is on the West wall of the Minster above the area now used as a shop. When it was erected in memory of Thomas by his elder brother who inherited the remaining estates, the area below was the Consistory Court of the Minster. Displayed beneath this monument is a skull and cross bones which indicates that the heir had predeceased the current holder of the baronetcy.

John, the eldest son was married to Frances Dodington and already had children by her when his father died including an heir, William, born around 1641. Unfortunately John did not outlive his father by very long. He died in late November 1661, his will being proved on 18th April 1662. His death caused a further election of the Governors of the Grammar School.

Charles II was restored, arriving in Britain on his 30th birthday, 29th May, 1660. There was public acclaim, church bells would have been rung and there were probably discreet parties held in the houses of committed royalists who would no doubt be planning revenge on those Parliamentarians who had taken their property during the Interregnum. The Book of Common Prayer was re-introduced. Weddings in church which had been forbidden were now re-introduced. The King's arms were quickly re-painted on the walls of the Minster.

William Hanham embarked on a considerable amount of building work on the Deans court property because by the time Hearth Tax was re-introduced in 1662 and a charge of 2d for each fire demanded, there were 24 hearths which suggests that a house with about thirty rooms existed. These would have been the rooms in which the family lived. The windows consisted of many small panes of glass which was still very expensive and not as clear as modern sheet glass. The rear windows may still have been shuttered.

It was the practice to have many household servants, most of whom were accommodated in small garret rooms below the eaves of the house.

Deans Court and the stewpond from the South. c.1880.

Cooks were usually male and ruled their kitchens with an iron skillet if no rod was available! There were separate stores for meat, fish, fruit and game, and another for dairy produce. Valuable items like spice and tea were kept under lock and key as was the master's wine cellar. A still room was used to make preserves such as chutney, jellies, brawn and store all the foods which needed the cold marble slab to set. Upstairs, including nursery staff and downstairs employees had their ranks and often a different livery. Outside there were stablemen, grooms, boot-boys and coachmen as well as gardeners, sawyers, and woodsmen.

When King Charles II visited Kingston Lacy in 1665, passing through Wimborne on 15th September, William was probably on the guest list of those invited to the nearby manor which had suffered so much in the Civil War. Everyone had heard of the suffering of Lady Mary Bankes and her family.

William Hanham purchased a baronetcy from the crown in 1667. He married Elizabeth Cooper, niece of Lord Ashley, 1st Earl of Shaftesbury, a local landowner and lord of Wimborne St Giles. She yearned to enter society as Lady Hanham. Gaining this title may well have been part of the marriage contract.

The manor court held at Deans Court

Their son Sir John Hanham came of age in 1690, but he too had little idea of economising and quickly got into debt. Fortunately he fell in love with Jane Eyre, of Neston Park in Wiltshire and was married in 1693, her father rescuing the financial situation.

King Charles had died in 1685 leaving his Catholic brother James to succeed him. Once again Catholicism was in the ascendancy. Priests at the Minster hastily adapted their services to the King's requirements and those who had persecuted foreign trained priests and Catholic landowners were out of favour. Dorset gentlemen were prime movers in issuing the invitation to the late king's sister to take the throne. On 15th November 1688 William and Mary of Orange landed and were crowned in February 1689.

As an ardent Catholic supporter of the now exiled King James II, Elizabeth Hanham, (née Cooper) found herself in the Tower of London accused of High Treason in 1689. She was not sentenced to death but remained under surveillance for the next five years.

Sir John Hanham of Deans Court died on 24th September 1709.

Sir William Hanham, 3rd Baronet married Mary Norris of Nonsuch in Wiltshire on 15th June 1717 when her father agreed to give the couple £3800.

The consistory court in a panelled corner of the Minster

In all the Hanhams had nine children. While his wife spent most of her time looking after the children Sir William set about re-building Deans Court in 1725. Roughly three quarters of the present building, 'L' shaped with frontages on both north and east sides, was from plans possibly prepared by the Bastard brothers from Blandford. Much of the foundation was based on the old Saxon Deanery. They used very small hand-made bricks and were renowned for their high quality pointing. A range of outbuildings were also constructed. Visitors will see the panelling installed at this time is still visible in the hall.

Sir William Hanham, 3rd Baronet as a child (left) & his siblings

In the course of his duties as Lord of the Manor of the Deanery, Sir William would have either attended the Manor Court himself or sent a steward. He would also renew leases and collect the heriot when sons inherited the father's cottage. He received the oath of loyalty of new tenants, supervised the election of the Hayward, the Ale Taster, the Constable and so on. One guess as to which position was most hotly contested! From the small sketch *(page 18)* the small paned windows, three on each side, are still there today.

Rev. Sir James Hanham, 6th Baronet & his son Rev. Sir James, 7th Baronet

When Sir William died suddenly on 28th March 1762 he had not written a will. Administration was granted to the two eldest sons, William now the 4th Baronet born in 1718 and James, born in 1725/26. They sold some of his possessions at auction in Wimborne the following August.

William had been to New College Oxford and married Anne, daughter of James and Jane Jennings. His mother in law came from the Constantine family of Merley on the Poole side of Wimborne. They had no children, Anne being buried in Wimborne in September 1756.

William, now a Lt. Col of the Dorset Militia, married again in 1762 the same year his father died. His second wife Mary was the daughter of William Lynch, Dean of Canterbury. Their only surviving child was William Thomas born in June the following year but Mary died in childbirth in October 1764. Sir William also held the title Deputy Lieutenant of Dorset.

Sir William's third wife was Harriott, daughter of Henry Drax of Charborough, another local landowner whose land abutted the turnpike. They had no children and he died in February 1776 leaving as his heir William Thomas, a minor.

While officiating at the Consistory Court of the Minster from 1768 onwards the senior man was referred to as 'Bishop', an epithet which lasted for the next seventy years. To a large extent this court dealt with the moral behaviour of the parishioners of Wimborne Minster.

Sir William Thomas Hanham, 5th baronet, took over many of his father's duties but died in 1791 aged only twenty eight. The title fell to his father's younger brother Reverend James, now the sixth baronet. Having little prospect of inheriting the estate he had gone into the priesthood. He rose to become the Minister of Wimborne Minster in 1754 and held the position until 1800. He married Jane, niece and sole heir of William Phelips of Corfe Mullen on 6th September 1757. She was given a huge dowry and the marriage was most certainly fruitful. They had five sons and eight daughters, the eldest James, born on 10th March 1760. Rev. Hanham died in 1806 just after his eightieth birthday, a great age.

His eldest son, also in the priesthood became the seventh baronet.

There is such a sad story of unrequited love between Reverend James (junior) and a young lady, Sarah Lester. They were in love but both fathers refused permission for the couple to marry. Being in 'trade' was still thought to be beneath the aspirations of the heir to a baronetcy. The young lovers were forced to look elsewhere for marriage partners.

Reverend James Hanham's first marriage on 16th April 1793 was to Ann, daughter of Lt. Edward Pike RN of Lytchet. They had four sons and two daughters. The eldest son James died aged only four and their second son Edward born in 1796 also died before reaching his teens. Two daughters survived.

William, the third son was born on 7th May 1798 and he inherited the baronetcy. Phelips the fourth son went into the church serving at Wimborne minster from 1829 to 1848, moved to a nearby parish but died without ever marrying four years later.

A gang of French prisoners of war were employed to build the famous serpentine wall at Deans Court during the Napoleonic wars. Within the walled garden fruit, vegetables and flowers were grown for the household. The wall on the far side abuts the old Grammar school which was re-built in the middle 1800s in the style of Henry VII whose mother, Margaret Beaufort, Countess of Richmond, had founded the first school for boys in Wimborne.

Reverend Sir James remained a widower for ten years then married Eliza Dean, daughter of Lt. William Patey on 14th December 1815. They had three sons and one daughter. James died shortly after becoming eighteen so John, who was born in 1823 eventually inherited Deans Court and future baronets later descended from him.

Reverend Sir James Hanham died on 2nd April 1849 was succeeded by Sir William as the 8th baronet who was both a sea captain and a cavalry officer in the militia. He had married but had no children and died in March 1877. Lacking a son, the next heir was Captain John, but he too died very suddenly. Captain John Hanham's death was both tragic and remarkable. He had fought in India and whilst under fire had rescued the regimental colours from a burning barge on the river Ganges. A charred fragment of the flag is preserved at Deans Court. He ended his career with the Depot Battalion at Preston.

Having disciplined an Irish soldier, Pte. McCaffery, the man's grievance obviously festered. On seeing Captain Hanham walking in the barrack square with the Colonel he fired one shot from a rifle. The single bullet passed through the Colonel and then fatally wounded Captain Hanham. The Colonel died immediately and Captain Hanham a few days later on 16th September 1861.

Stained glass wimdow, Deans Court

Altar frontal with semi-precious stones embroidered by Amy Hanham

After his death his widow Amy and their children, John, the heir to the title, Amy, Phelips Brook and Eliza Frances, continued living at Deans Court. The widow painted her bedroom in mauve, the traditional colour for mourning. She was a very accomplished needlewoman and many of her covers, screens and bedspreads are still in use today.

Crewelwork curtains and pelmets made by Amy Hanham in the Drawing Room

John Alexander Hanham 9th Bart succeeded, being Captain Hanham's half-brother, but because the estate had been divided between Captain Hanham's four children under the laws of intestacy, found it difficult to live at Deans Court. John had graduated from Oxford University as a Master of Arts. He was called to the Bar in 1881, served a term as Deputy Lieutenant of Dorset and was a Justice of the Peace.

Sir John Alexander was appointed the Apparitor-General for the Province and Diocese of Canterbury in 1885 assisting in the consecration of Bishops. He threw down the gauntlet to challenge anyone to declare that the bishop about to be consecrated is not a fit and worthy person.

Portrait of Captain John Hanham
painted posthumously by his widow Amy

He married Cordelia Lopes, daughter of Judge Lord Ludlow of Heywood inheriting a fortune on her father's death. They had three children:- Cordelia Amy Maud, John Ludlow born on 23rd January 1898 and Henry Phelips born on 6th April 1901. Both the boys would inherit the Baronetcy in their turn.

In 1887 land was needed for a hospital. Sir John gave some pasture land by the Chain Gate toll gate close to St Margaret's chapel and almshouses, which used to be a leper hospital in medieval times. The new hospital was built in celebration of Queen Victoria's Golden Jubilee.

Sir John Alexander Hanham died on 21st February 1911. The funeral at the Minster on 27th was crowded. He had succeeded to the title of 9th Bart in 1877 and followed a career in law like many of his ancestors. Subsequent to her late husband's gift of land for the new hospital building, the Hon Lady Hanham provided a new operating table and paid for electricity to be installed in the operating theatre.

Sir John Ludlow Hanham 10th baronet

Sir John Ludlow Hanham being the eldest son succeeded to the baronetcy and was the 10th of that title. Born in the beginning of 1898 he was only thirteen years old and may have had trustees in addition to his mother to assist in running the estate. He served during WWI as a Captain in the Grenadier Guards and was wounded. The photograph above was taken in 1919, the year he came of age.

After this he was Aide de Camp to his uncle Viscount Bledisloe, Governor of New Zealand for two years. He too entered the law and was called to the Bar at the Inner Temple. He also served in WWII before becoming Deputy Lieutenant for the County of Dorset. He too held the office of Apparitor General for the Diocese and Province of Canterbury, challenging the crowd on the steps of St Mary le Bow church on 26th November, 1928. This same year Sir John took the opportunity to join an Oxford University expedition to Greenland. He and his younger brother Henry kept a diary and returned home with two polar bear skins which can be seen in the house. His sudden death on 30th April 1955 aged only 57 was deemed to be a great loss to Wimborne and the wider community. His younger brother, Henry Phelips Hanham became the 11th Baronet aged fifty four. In WWII he was an officer with the Royal Artillery. He died in November 1973 without having married.

The title therefore was inherited by a distant cousin, Sir Michael William Hanham who became the 12th baronet. Born in 1922, his grandfather was Col. Phelips Hanham JP., the younger brother of Sir John Alexander Hanham, 9th baronet. Educated at Winchester, Michael Hanham joined the RAF and was awarded the Distinguished Flying Cross for fifty five sorties in Lancaster bombers. He married Margaret Jane in 1954 and spent more than thirty years restoring the house and gardens. They both had a great interest in the well-being of the soil and took advantage of the existence of the walled garden.

They created a vegetable sanctuary, re-introducing vegetables from the past. Fruit and nut trees may even be descended from those planted by nuns and monks centuries ago. In 2009 when Sir Michael died, the present occupant of Deans Court inherited the baronetcy being the 13th to hold the title.

Portraits of Sir Michael Hanham and Lady Jane Hanham by Carl Cheek

Sir William, born in 1957, ran a successful fine art business until the estate claimed his full attention. Two world wars and great changes in technology and farming methods have forced the introduction of up-to-date management techniques thereby ensuring the long term survival of Deans Court. Together with his wife Lady Alison, the house and garden continue to thrive. A busy café and homeware shop complement the increased public access to the oldest house in Wimborne and certainly the house with the longest and most varied history in the town.

Room Guide

Today's accommodation is arranged for family living and greater comfort. The Hall used to be the largest room before the major alterations in 1725. It still has a high ceiling with a fireplace wide enough to accommodate the sweep's boys who had to climb the 50ft chimney. Much of the panelling from this period is still intact as are the coats of arms installed in the windows. Huge double doors connect to the other rooms on the ground floor and a double archway cut through the thick Saxon wall leads to one of the staircases.

The Hall, Deans Court

The Dining Room contains a sequence of family portraits. A huge Victorian dining table seating more than twenty people dominates the centre surrounded by objets d'art. The windows are of spun glass supported by glazing bars installed in 1760s before the introduction of Window Tax.

The Kitchen was once the room used as the Deanery Court. It has been subdivided for modern living but used to be more than 30ft long and had three large windows on each side like the dimensions of the Dining Room on the opposite side of the entrance Hall.

The library is a cosier room with an unusual break-front cabinet housing an eclectic selection of books. In addition to those which reflect the interests of past members of the family there are two copies of Hutchin's History of Dorset from the late 18th century, gardening and natural history tomes and a book on Chinese torture! A unique Bell chair is beside the bookcase. Made from surplus wood when extra bells were hung in the Minster during its Victorian 'restoration', each Governor of the Grammar School received one.

In the 1930s the fashionable company Liberty's were commissioned to redecorate some rooms. In the Morning Room, because of possible dampness the wallpaper is stretched and suspended on battens to keep it off the wall. When water did spoilt it, Sir Michael and Lady Jane carefully cut out each of the Gothic crosses and stuck them on replacement paper so that to the casual observer no difference can be detected.

The vast cellars below the house had rooms for the housekeeper and the butler alongside the larder, dairy, wine cellar and servants' hall. Store rooms for meat and vegetables together with a still room meant that all domestic activities took place 'below stairs'. The cellar walls are those of the Saxon building, the spiral staircase ascending from within the thickness of these walls up to the attic servants' quarters at the top. More recently a paint scheme of dark blue and cream was introduced to warn guests if they strayed into the working areas. These colours may have been the same as the servants' livery.

The nursery which saw generations of the Hanham family grow had rooms nearby for the nursery maids and the governess who taught the children. The toys of many boys and girls were discovered in the cupboards when the present baronet moved in with his parents in the mid 1970's.

Guests of course used the staircase of cantilevered Purbeck marble steps with a wrought iron balustrade made in the 1760s. Some of the bedrooms are still furnished with period furniture together with many of the hangings and unique needlework done by Amy Hanham, wife of John Hanham who was murdered at Preston. She embroidered covers, made tapestry fire screens and spent over forty years embroidering an altar frontal with semi-precious stones for Wimborne Minster, which is still in use today.

The cantilevered staircase, c.1760

Some cupboards have been renovated during Victorian times, the ornate fronts being attached to plain wood frames. Many windows still use old glass but even with a mild distortion, the views of the garden and the river Stour are superb, especially when the huge magnolia and other bushes are flowering.

Deans Court is truly a house of antiquity, each room and corner revealing the character of its occupants throughout its long history.

Janet K L Seal - *Brought up in Lancashire, Jan went to boarding school in Wales then a language college in Switzerland. Skiing figured largely in free time, the nearest slopes a short distance from the classroom! Secretarial college in London was the final tranche of education, the skill of touch typing proving extremely useful in later life. In 1990 Jan and her husband bought the site of an old manor house NE of Wimborne. Research proved that records for 'Uddens' go back to Saxon times.*

Using more than twenty-five years of investigation into the past Jan has written several historical novels about the manor and Wimborne, 'The King's Chalice' trilogy, published by Bretwalda Books. 'The History, Myths & Legends of Colehill', the high ground above the town, has just been published. Jan volunteers at the local community run library, cares for her retired horse, gives talks and continues her research into the history of Wimborne.